BURIED *in* ICE

THE MYSTERY OF A LOST ARCTIC EXPEDITION

First published in Canada by
Random House of Canada Ltd.,
1265 Aerowood Drive, Mississauga, Ontario L4W 1B9

Canadian Cataloguing in Publication Data
Beattie, Owen
  Buried in ice

(Time quest series)
ISBN 0-394-22258-X

1. Franklin, John, Sir, 1786-1847 — Juvenile literature.
2. Arctic regions — Discovery and exploration — British —
Juvenile literature. 3. Archaeological expeditions — Canada,
Northern — Juvenile literature. I. Geiger, John, 1960-   .
II. Title. III. Series: A Time quest book (Mississauga, Ont.).
FC3961.3.B43 1992   917.19'5041'092   C91-094515-2
G670.1981.F73B43 1992

Design & Art Direction: Gordon Sibley Design Inc.
Illustration: Janet Wilson
Maps and Diagrams: Jack McMaster
Editorial Director: Hugh M. Brewster
Project Editors: Nan Froman, Mireille Majoor
Production Director: Susan Barrable
Production Assistant: Donna Chong
Color Separation: Colour Technologies
Printer: Friesen Printers

Endpapers: Huge icebergs tower above a lone ship
in this fanciful Victorian engraving.

Previous page: British sailors explore the many
wonders of the Arctic in the 1800s.

Right: An Arctic exploring ship caught between
massive ice floes could be crushed in minutes.

Overleaf: The *Investigator* was one of many ships
sent in search of Franklin's expedition.

Produced by Madison Press Books
40 Madison Avenue
Toronto, Ontario
Canada M5R 2S1   *Printed in Canada*

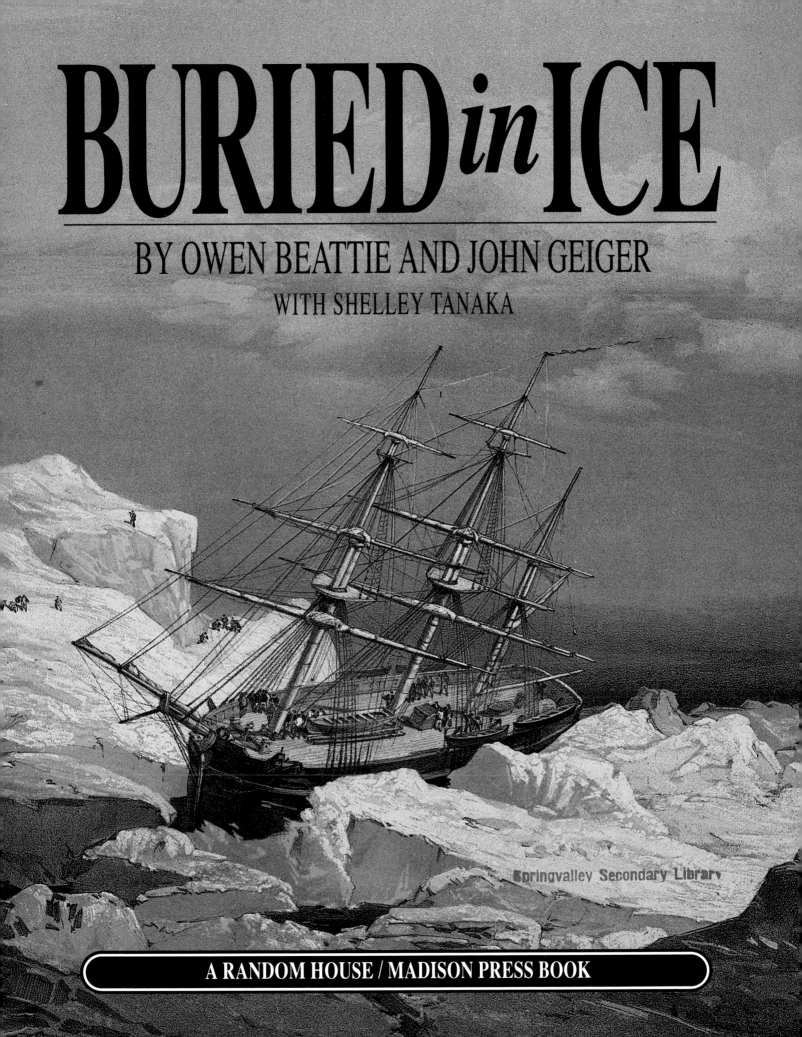

BURIED *in* ICE

BY OWEN BEATTIE AND JOHN GEIGER

WITH SHELLEY TANAKA

A RANDOM HOUSE / MADISON PRESS BOOK

CONTENTS

For Megan, Jennifer and Matthew — Owen Beattie
For Annie — John Geiger

It was a quest that lured men to their graves. For centuries explorers had dreamed of finding a ship route to the riches of Asia across the ice-choked seas above North America. Again and again ships would sail for the Arctic—only to be trapped for long, dark months in a world of soaring ice mountains and eerie lights. In the spring of 1845 it seemed as if nothing could stop Sir John Franklin's lavishly equipped expedition from finding the Northwest Passage. Crowds cheered and waved as the two ships sailed from England. But not one of Franklin's men would ever return home alive.

lues to the mysterious disappearance of Sir John Franklin and his men had been slowly pieced together over the years. Now anthropologist Owen Beattie thinks he knows why things went so terribly wrong on that doomed expedition. But he needs evidence to prove his theory. Beneath the permafrost of Beechey Island lie the bodies of three of Franklin's sailors. Can they help him solve the mystery of why two ships and 129 men vanished into the icy blackness at the top of the world?

CHAPTER ONE

THE FRANKLIN MYSTERY

Beechey Island, Canadian Arctic, August 1984

"I can see the graves!" I shouted to the pilot of the Twin Otter as we approached Beechey Island. Two thousand feet below, the tiny dark points on the gravel-covered island could only be one thing—the grave markers of three young sailors who had died on Sir John Franklin's expedition.

Soon I could see other items that had been left there by Franklin's crew 138 years before. They had spent the winter of 1845-46 here when their ships were locked in an ice-filled bay off the island's east coast. I could make out a ruined storehouse, a large pile of food tin cans, and the outlines of where campsites and the carpenter's work area had been. I could also see large round pits in the gray gravel. These had been dug by search parties looking for clues to the fate of the Franklin expedition in the early 1850s. "They look just like bomb craters," I said to the pilot as the plane circled in preparation for landing.

The pilot put the plane down on a beach ridge right next to the graves. We lurched and rocked over the uneven ground, stopping not far from the little graveyard. The pilot shut down the left engine—the noise of the still-running right engine was a reminder that we had to hurry to unload our supplies.

Quickly unstrapping our seatbelts, we moved in a single file to the back of the plane. The door flew open and the five of us jumped to the ground and began unloading the ton of equipment that would support us for the next three weeks.

When the last crate had been unloaded, the pilot started the left engine and prepared for take-off. We moved up the beach to a safe distance and watched the plane accelerate, then bump into the air with a loud roar.

I walked over to the graves that I had flown so far to see and bent down to decipher the inscription traced on the weathered surface of the first headstone: "Sacred to the Memory of John Torrington who departed this life January 1st A.D. 1846, on board of H.M. ship *Terror* aged 20 years."

In the distance I could hear the sound of the engines of the departing Twin Otter quietly fade into the distance. Farther along the beach

From the Twin Otter *(right)* I could see the graves of three of Franklin's sailors and those of two other men who died in the search for the missing ships *(above)*.

the four other members of our research team were setting up camp, surrounded by a mountain of boxes, tents, excavation equipment and supplies.

It was very quiet. In the Arctic you can feel more alone than anywhere else on this planet. Against the desolate stretch of gravel shore, the three headstones stood out clearly in the summer sunlight. Buried alongside John Torrington were Able-bodied Seaman John Hartnell and Royal Marine Private William Braine.

Because he died early in the expedition *(inset)*, John Torrington was not one of those forced to leave the ships to begin a doomed southward march *(above)*.

The graves were a powerful reminder of the dangers of Arctic exploration. These men were the astronauts of their time, willing to risk everything in the name of science and adventure, and for the glory of the British Empire. Had they conquered the Northwest Passage, they would have been hailed as heroes. Instead they lay buried on an icy shore thousands of miles from home.

In 1845 Sir John Franklin set out from England in search of the Northwest Passage. For over three hundred years, sailors had tried to find this sea route north of the Canadian mainland, which they believed linked the Atlantic and Pacific oceans. There would be great honor and glory for those who discovered the way.

But Franklin's two ships, the *Erebus* and the *Terror*, became trapped in the iron-tight grip of the Arctic ice. After two years, his men were finally forced to abandon their dreams of discovery and desert their ships in a last desperate struggle for survival.

Their frozen ordeal led to the greatest rescue mission ever attempted. Dozens of ships and hundreds of men from all over Europe and America raced into uncharted Arctic waters in an effort to find the expedition. But the searchers were chasing phantoms. Many of Franklin's

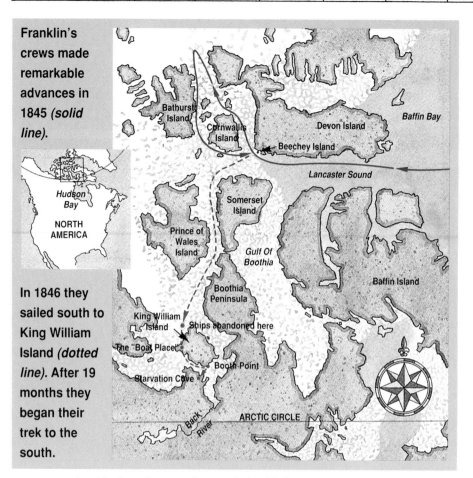

Franklin's crews made remarkable advances in 1845 *(solid line)*.

In 1846 they sailed south to King William Island *(dotted line)*. After 19 months they began their trek to the south.

During all of these searches a number of grisly discoveries were made when the scattered bones from some of Franklin's men were found. But the biggest question remained unanswered. How could the greatest Arctic expedition of all time have ended in such tragedy? Why had Franklin's men died? I had come to Beechey Island to find out. With my skills as a physical anthropologist I hoped to solve these mysteries. I could investigate the causes of the disaster by analyzing human remains from the lost expedition.

In 1981 I had gone to King William Island in search of the bones of some of Franklin's missing men. We knew that in 1869 several Inuit had reported seeing the remains of a white man on the southern shore.

men were dead before the search vessels had left port.

Yet even after it was clear that Franklin's men had perished, the hunt continued. Years later the searchers were still coming—in 1859, in 1869, in 1879, in 1931 and in 1967. These men were no longer looking for any survivors. Too many years had passed for that to be possible. Instead, they were looking for clues to what could have gone so terribly wrong: written records, the ships' log books, maybe even the remains of Franklin's ships.

On our second day on the island one of the research assistants, Karen Digby, had walked up to me. She was cradling something in her hands. It looked like a broken china bowl.

"Is it human?" she asked, handing it to me.

"Fantastic!" I cried. All I needed was one look to know. She had found a fragment of a human skull.

For the rest of the day we all combed the area and gradually collected thirty-one fragments of a human skeleton. It came to be known by our team as the Booth Point skeleton.

By carefully studying the shape of the skull's frontal bone and features around the eye sockets, I could see that it belonged to a Caucasian. Heavy brow ridges on the skull and well-developed muscle markings on the limb bones identified the person as male. He had been young at the time of his death, between twenty and twenty-five years old.

There was no doubt. This was the final resting place for one of Sir John Franklin's brave sailors.

Back in the laboratory in Edmonton, I examined the bones more closely. "Scurvy," I commented to a colleague. "There's little doubt that he suffered from

This pile of bones from Franklin's sailors was found on King William Island in 1931.

scurvy." I could clearly see the unnatural pitting and scaling on the outer surface of the bone caused by the disease.

Fresh fruit and vegetables, a main source of vitamin C, could not last on long sea voyages. Scurvy, caused by a lack of this vitamin, plagued European sailors for centuries. It was a dreadful illness that resulted in loose teeth, bleeding gums, sore joints, weight loss, exhaustion and even death. If the disease became widespread among a crew, the ship might be unable to function.

For years people blamed scurvy and starvation for the disastrous end of the Franklin expedition, and the bones I was examining certainly indicated that scurvy was a factor. But I wondered what else I might discover.

We explored King William Island on foot and by canoe *(above)*. It was here we found bones from the foot of one of Franklin's sailors *(inset)*.

As part of my analysis, I submitted small samples of the sailor's bone for element testing, a scientific process that measures the presence and amounts of a number of different elements contained in human bone.

I was astonished by what the tests revealed—high levels of lead. In fact, there was so much lead in the bone that it was probable that this sailor had been poisoned by it.

Lead is a metal that is very dangerous when eaten or inhaled. In large enough doses it can even kill a person. Smaller amounts damage certain organs in the body and can interfere with how people think and behave. A person can actually go mad from the effects of lead.

Had this sailor taken in the lead during the voyage or before? Had other members of the expedition also suffered from deadly amounts of this metal?

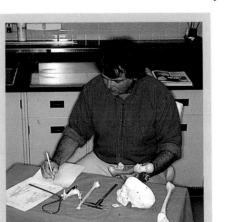

By studying bones we can learn how people in the past lived and died. Tests of the bones we found in the Arctic showed levels of lead that were unusually high. I wondered whether all of Franklin's men might have had lead in their bodies.

To answer these questions I needed more than just skeletal remains, since bone analysis alone couldn't tell me how recently a person had been exposed to lead. What I needed to examine was soft tissue—skin, muscle, hair and organs from members of Franklin's doomed crew.

I knew there was only one place where I had a chance of finding such tissues preserved in the frozen Arctic ground. And so I had come to inspect the three graves that had been dug almost 140 years ago on the shores of Beechey Island.

As I walked back to help my friends set up camp, I wondered what our investigation would tell us about John Torrington and his shipmates. Would we find any more clues to the puzzle of what had happened to Sir John Franklin and the rest of his men?

SETTING SAIL FOR THE ARCTIC

Greenhithe, England, May 19, 1845

"I wouldn't change places with the richest man in the world today!" John Torrington took his clay pipe out of his mouth and grinned at Luke Smith.

Luke smiled back and nodded hesitantly. The two young men stood at the rail of the upper deck of the H.M.S. *Terror*, watching the waving crowds on shore.

Luke had to admit, he was excited. The docks were crowded with people who watched as the final supplies were loaded onto the *Terror* and her sister ship, the *Erebus*. Soon the ships would weigh anchor and travel down the River Thames—and then across the Atlantic Ocean to the Canadian Arctic, one of the last unexplored territories in the world. Families and friends were cheering and crying as final goodbyes were said to the 134 crew members from both ships. Somewhere in the crowd were Luke's aunt and uncle, whom he had lived with since his parents had died two years earlier.

His uncle was even more excited about the trip than he was, Luke thought ruefully. The man had pulled a lot of strings to get his nineteen-year-old nephew taken on as a stoker on board the *Terror*. Many of the crew members had already sailed to distant parts of the world. Even John, who was also only nineteen, knew all about Arctic travel. At least, that's what he told Luke.

Now they were about to set sail on the biggest adventure of their lives.

The *Erebus* and *Terror* leaving England. Everyone expected them to chart a course through the Arctic within a year.

"We're going to discover a new boat passage right across the top of the world," John said grandly as he straightened the white and blue kerchief that he wore knotted around his neck. Luke knew it had been a farewell gift from his father and stepmother. "Do you know what that means? By autumn we could be heading across the Pacific Ocean, sailing to the Orient. We'll be exploring land and seas that no man has ever seen before."

"I thought you said that there were people already living in the Arctic," Luke said. "The people they call Eskimos."

John waved his pipe dismissively. "Oh, sure," he said. "And we'll see polar bears and seals and walruses, too. But these are *Parts Unknown*. We'll be the first white men to explore this land. After our voyage, the map of the world will be changed forever."

Luke nodded. It was a privilege, to be sure. But he wished he had even a fraction of John's self-confidence. Instead, Luke wasn't really certain that he wanted to be here. He had heard too many stories about the perils of sailing the icy seas of the north. Just a week ago he had seen a cartoon in a newspaper showing an iceberg

Right: **John confidently describes to Luke what they can expect to see once the ships reach the Arctic.**

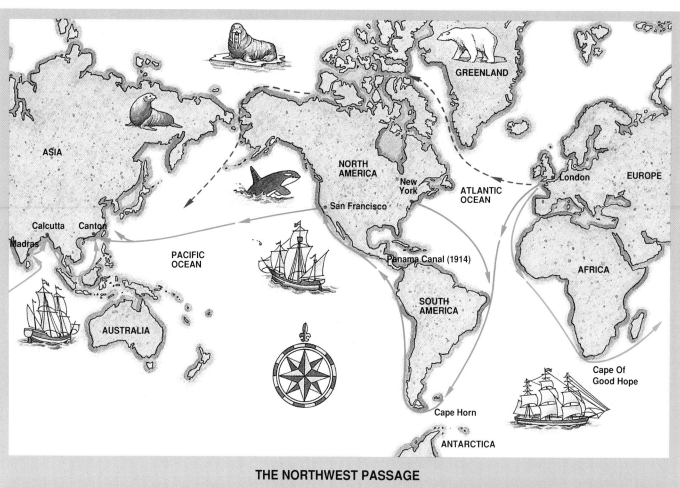

THE NORTHWEST PASSAGE

In 1845 ship voyages to the Pacific were long and dangerous. European ships sailed around Africa to ports such as Madras and Calcutta in India, and Canton in China *(blue line)*. American and European ships traveled around the tip of South America to San Francisco *(green line)* and some of the vessels went on from there to China. The British dreamed of finding a shortcut across the icy seas north of Canada *(dotted line)* and hundreds of men died trying to find the Northwest Passage. It was not until 1914 when the Panama Canal was cut through Central America that the first real shortcut to Asia was made possible.

shaped like a grinning skeleton of death, waiting to devour a tiny ship.

The ship in the picture hadn't looked much different from the ones they were sailing in now, he thought suddenly. Both the *Erebus* and the *Terror* looked just like stubby little black and yellow washtubs rigged with sails.

"Do you think the ships are up to it?" he asked John.

"Give me one of these sturdy vessels over those fancy new American clipper ships any day," John snorted. "These are old navy warships. Why, they've even hammered sheets of iron onto the bows of these old ladies. They'll plow through that Arctic ice like a knife through butter, just wait and see."

Luke laughed. He hadn't known John for long, but already he realized his new friend had a tendency to exaggerate. Still, he was glad they would be working together. At least things wouldn't be dull.

John had been appointed chief stoker in charge of the *Terror*'s steam engine and boiler, and Luke was one of the stokers who would be working with him. The two of them, along with the third stoker, William Johnson, wouldn't have much to do until the ships were in Arctic waters. Two tugboats would pull the ships out of the Thames and up the east coast of England and Scotland, and then the winds would fill their sails and carry them across the Atlantic, just as they had carried thousands of voyagers since Christopher Columbus's time.

John ran his hand over the *Terror*'s wooden rail, which had been freshly painted. "This ship has proven her worth in the Arctic before," he said. "She's been tossed forty feet up the side of a huge iceberg and lived to tell the tale. Besides, both ships have been outfitted with the very latest equipment. We even have hot water heaters running under the deck, did you know that?"

Luke nodded. His uncle had already described the well-equipped vessel down to the smallest detail.

"We'll be living as well as Queen Victoria herself," John went on, ignoring Luke's nod. "Fancy silverware and fine china and mahogany writing desks for the officers. We're taking a little piece of England to the other side of the world. I even hear there's an organ on board, and a library filled with over a thousand books."

Luke shrugged. "It doesn't matter to me," he said quietly. "I can't read."

John clapped him on the back and laughed. "Well, you'll have plenty of time to learn. They give lessons on board, but I can teach you myself. It'll probably be much faster. Here, let me show you something." John quickly looked around him then pulled a small notebook out of his shirt. "I'm going to keep a record of everything that happens on this trip, and when we get back to England, I'll be able to sell my account to a newspaper," he whispered. He nudged Luke and grinned, and his straight white teeth gleamed with mischief.

Luke looked at John doubtfully. He knew that keeping a secret journal was against regulations. The sailors had been ordered to give all notes and journals to the captain after the voyage.

A burst of shouting and applause erupted from the dock, and both young men straightened as they watched Sir John Franklin stride toward the ships. Sir John was accompanied by his officers, his wife, Lady Jane Franklin, and his daughter, Eleanor.

Sir John Franklin, shown here as a young man, was one of the best-known Arctic explorers of his day. Tales of his adventures and narrow escapes made him a hero in England. At the age of fifty-nine he was offered command of the 1845 expedition even though his last journey north had been 17 years before.

This was Luke's first glimpse of their commander, and he couldn't help being disappointed. Sir John was a beefy, jowly man with a thick neck, and he looked vaguely pale and nervous now, dwarfed by the crush of his family and officers.

"Isn't he a little too old to be making such a hard voyage?" Luke asked John. "My aunt said a sixty-year-old man shouldn't —"

"Fifty-nine, mate," John interrupted briskly. "Sir John is only fifty-nine, and you couldn't have a better man at the helm. He has fought Napoleon and been shipwrecked in the South Pacific and sailed all over the world. And he's already been to the Arctic three times. The second time, he was there for three years, and he only missed starving to death by eating his own boots."

Luke looked at his friend sharply. Was John joking? Sometimes it was hard to tell.

"Not that starving's going to be a worry for us," John continued. "We're taking enough food to last for three years—five if we bag the odd polar bear. But the voyage won't take that long. We'll be up to our elbows in Chinese pearls and silks within a year."

Luke watched as Sir John talked with Captain Francis Crozier, the tall Irishman who would pilot the *Terror*. Sir John and Commander James Fitzjames would be in charge of the *Erebus*.

Beside her husband, Lady Franklin looked small and anxious. She never took her gaze off him, but Lady Eleanor, who appeared to be about twenty, was staring around at the goings on with a great deal of curiosity.

Luke stood a little taller. John was right. How could he feel anything but courageous and proud at a great moment like this. The British were destined to conquer the Northwest Passage, no matter how forbidding it was. And he, Luke Smith, was proud to do his small part for the mighty navy of the British Empire. With the fearless Sir John Franklin as their leader, they were part of the greatest voyage of discovery that Britain had ever known.

T wo nights later, the *Terror* lurched and rolled off the coast of northern Scotland, as Luke and John wandered through the lower deck searching for a place to sling their hammocks.

Not quite a floating palace, Luke thought. Somewhere in the ship, he knew, officers were pouring each other another glass of wine, but for the crewmen, the evening brought only a nightly search for a place to sleep.

"When I'm an officer, I'll have my own cabin," John said crossly as he pushed his way past another sleeping

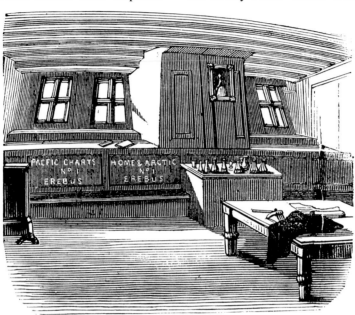

Sir John Franklin's large private cabin was very different from the cramped quarters occupied by the crew.

sailor. "They say that Sir John has huge quarters on the *Erebus*, but I would settle for Captain Crozier's cabin. No fuss for me."

In the forward mess, several other men were already sleeping. In the dim light of his candle, John found a spot between two benches. Luke gazed around at the lumpy dark shapes of sailors swaying rhythmically in the heavy seas. There was a spot over in the corner beside Thomas Burt, the ship's armorer. If he could attach one end of his hammock to Burt's hook, there would be room for him.

Luke carefully leaned over Burt's head to reach the hook. As he did, a sudden sharp lurch of the ship made him lose his footing and brought him staring into the angry eyeballs of the burly man.

"Here, watch it, boy."

Luke scrambled into his hammock and turned his back to Burt's glare.

But he couldn't sleep. The creaking of the *Terror*'s beams was bone-jarring. Luke lay on his back, staring up at the deck beams and trying to pretend he was back in his familiar bed at home.

He thought it was his imagination at first. There was an itchy feeling on his head. He reached up and felt his hair, then something furry, and a long, leathery, snake-like tail—

"Ow!" Something nipped his hand. He sat up, and heard the dull thud of a rat hitting the floor and then scurrying away.

Luke sighed. John had warned him about the rats that invaded every nook and cranny of the ship. John said they would chew the clothes right off your body if you let them. After a while, his friend explained, you could feel the tell-tale vibration their feet made as they

Right: **A horrified Luke discovers that he is sharing his hammock with a rat.**

climbed down the ropes of the hammock toward your head, and soon you learned how to swipe them off the rope without even waking up.

Luke shivered at the thought. It was going to be a long night.

He didn't know how long he had been sleeping before a spine-chilling howl jolted him awake. The scream was right beside his ear; it sounded as if it were coming from inside his own head. Luke sat up in the pitch blackness, trying to remember for a second where he was.

"What the—" From the other side of the mess, John's voice rang out, and a candle was lit.

Every four hours sailors were summoned from their hammocks to stand watch on the icy deck.

This medicine chest was found near a boat abandoned by Franklin's men. It still contained many of the powders and pills the ship's doctors would have prescribed for ill sailors.

Next to Luke, Thomas Burt was whimpering like a wounded animal.

As Luke struggled to get out of his hammock, his foot hit something hard. Burt screamed again, and this time his cry brought the other men running.

A heavy barrel filled with lemon juice had broken free from its tiedown. With the noise of the wind outside, no one had heard anything until the man's scream of pain. Burt's left leg was dangling over the hammock near the ground, pinned fast by the barrel. In the flickering light Luke could see Burt's grimacing face as he clutched the upper part of his leg between his hands.

It took three big men to roll the barrel back to its place and secure it with rope. By then, one of the ship's surgeons, John Peddie, had arrived.

As Luke and the others looked on silently, the doctor quickly took his surgical scissors out of his bag and cut apart Burt's trouser leg. When Peddie gently peeled back the trousers, Luke could see the mangled and bloody leg beneath.

"It's broken," said the doctor, looking right into Burt's face and shaking his head. "If you stay on the ship, there is every possibility that your leg will become badly infected. You could die. As it is, I don't know whether they can get you back in time to save the leg, but it's your only chance." Peddie looked around at the other men. "At least his timing is good. The tugboats are turning back tomorrow. Now someone help me get this man into sick bay."

Burt twitched in pain as the men lifted him. When they were gone, Luke looked at the man's empty hammock, swinging limply now. On the wooden planks below,

blood was already drying.

Luke looked at the barrel, now fastened securely back in place. If he had been sleeping in Burt's place, that could have been his leg crushed under that barrel. He might be the one sailing home tomorrow, back to firm land, his old room in his uncle's house, his aunt's delicious cooking...

"Poor fool," John muttered, shaking his head as he picked up the candle and made his way back to his hammock. "Burt will be sitting back in England with one leg, and he won't even have anything to show for it. He's going to miss everything—the adventure, and the

Franklin was not the first man to take the _Erebus_ and _Terror_ into polar waters. In 1839 Sir James Clark Ross sailed the two ships to Antarctica.

glory. Thank God it wasn't one of us."

Luke nodded silently as he crawled back into his hammock. Was Thomas Burt the unfortunate one? Such an unexpected disaster so early in the voyage just didn't seem right.

Tomorrow the ships would turn their bowsprits away from England for good. Luke wished he felt more sure that they would be coming back.

CHAPTER THREE

SICK BAY

Atlantic Ocean, June 16, 1845

Luke made his way through the forward mess. Out of habit, he held onto the edge of a table as he walked, even though the sea was calm today. It was a welcome change. For the past week the wind had been high, the ocean a never-ending succession of long and lofty rollers. Even the seasoned sailors had been seasick, so Luke hadn't felt so bad about the many times he had hung over the rail in the past few days, vomiting until he was almost too weak to stand up.

The older sailors had reassured him that the seasickness would pass, and they had been right. He felt fine now. He only wished the same thing were true for John Torrington.

Luke opened a tin of meat and one of potatoes and spooned some of each into a bowl. His mouth watered just looking at it, but the food was for John, not him.

John hadn't been feeling well for almost a week now. Two other sailors were also sick, but the ship's surgeons could not understand what was ailing them. The surgeons had ordered the sick men special rations of tinned food to try to build up their strength, but so far nothing seemed to be helping.

Luke carried the plate into sick bay. The other sick crew members were sleeping, but John lay in one of the beds staring at the ceiling. When he saw Luke, he smiled and raised himself up awkwardly on one elbow.

"Look what I've brought," Luke said cheerfully. "The doctor has ordered tinned food for you, while us poor peasants gnaw on salt fish and hard biscuits day after day. You're eating as well as Sir John himself. The rest of us probably won't even get a taste of the tinned goods until we're in the middle of the Arctic and the regular supplies have run out."

John's smile was wide. "Give it here. I might as well enjoy it. I'll be joining you fellows in those wormy seamen's rations soon enough, you know. I'll be up and about tomorrow." He struggled into a sitting position, and Luke handed him the dish. John began to shovel spoonfuls into his mouth, but Luke soon noticed that he was pushing the food around more than he was eating it.

"No good?" he asked anxiously.

John looked at him, annoyed. "Of course it's good," he said. He squinted at his dish. "I'm just not that fond of...potatoes, that's all."

The two stopped talking at the sound of deep voices outside the door. To their surprise, both Commander Fitzjames and Captain Crozier walked in, accompanied

Above: The elaborate lid from one of the hundreds of tins of potatoes carried by Franklin's ships. *Right:* Surgeon Peddie brings the ships' officers to visit John in sick bay.

by the ship's surgeons. John sat up a little straighter and brushed the hair back off his face. This was a rare occasion. Commander Fitzjames must have rowed across from the *Erebus*.

"These men have been ill for a few days, Captain, but I expect that situation to change soon," Surgeon Peddie explained. "It's far too early in the voyage for them to be suffering from scurvy, but I've ordered extra rations of tinned vegetables for them to eat just in case."

Commander Fitzjames frowned. "It is very odd," he said. "We have four men in sick bay as well. Perhaps just an extended bout of seasickness?"

Luke could see John's eyes widen with outrage, but the doctor shook his head.

"The stomach pain is unusual. Besides, these men are all experienced sailors, and I doubt that—"

Captain Crozier broke in. "Well, feed them back to health, Mr. Peddie." He looked at John steadily. "We'll be in Arctic waters soon, and it would help to have our chief stoker back in the engine room."

Before John could say anything, the group of officers had turned and left the room.

As soon as their footsteps grew faint, John's body sagged slightly, but he continued to eat. When he was finished, he handed his dish to Luke. "If eating is the cure, then I'll eat. Get me some more."

As Luke and John climbed the steps to the maindeck, the screeching of gulls filled the air over their heads. The ships were anchored in a protected channel at Disco Island off the west coast of Greenland. It had been almost eight weeks since they left England.

Slowly, the two sailors walked over to the rail. In the gray light of the overcast sky, John looked paler than usual, but his eyes gleamed as he took in the rugged, desolate landscape around them. On the island, men were collecting eider duck eggs, while others were preparing to slaughter the last of the live oxen for fresh meat. Nearby, the supply ship that had sailed with them, the *Barretto Junior*, was lashed alongside the *Erebus*, and several crewmen were busy transferring her stores onto the ship. Soon the supply vessel would return to England, leaving the two

The two ships stopped in Greenland to take on a final load of fuel and supplies before sailing into the Canadian Arctic.

little ships to go on alone.

The expedition had been in the Davis Strait for nearly two weeks, and on the days when John wasn't feeling well, Luke would go below to tell him what was happening above deck. Already they had seen a large group of bottle-nosed whales plunging and frolicking nearby. On one day, over sixty drifting icebergs had been spotted by the lookouts, their sides sculpted smooth, their tops crusty. Nearly a hundred walruses had swarmed around the two ships, tumbling, diving and splashing with their flippers and tails.

John had been eager for every scrap of news that Luke brought him, and he quickly wrote it all down in his journal. "You're my eyes," he would tell Luke. "When we get back to England and I sell this account, I'll split the money with you. Maybe you could do some sketches to go with it."

Luke smiled. He was quite a good draftsman, much better at drawing than John was. He had taken to spending many evenings in the ship's library, drawing the birds and landscape he had seen that day. On other nights, if he was feeling well enough, John would spend

Above: Icebergs and walruses *(inset)* can be seen all year long in the icy waters off the coast of Greenland.

a few hours teaching him how to read and write.

"The air," John said happily. "I could drink it, it smells so good." He took a deep breath, but instantly bent over in a fit of coughing that came from deep within his chest.

Luke clutched his friend's shoulders. "Maybe we should go back down," he said, trying to keep the concern out of his voice. For the past few weeks he had thought that John was getting better. John had even managed to work in the steam room for several days. But now Luke could see just how drawn and thin his friend was. Even after three solid weeks of tinned meat and soup and vegetables, John's small frame seemed to disappear inside the new winter clothing that had been distributed to the crew.

John shook his head vigorously. "No!" he rasped. There were tears in his eyes from the effort of holding back his cough. "I've been buried down in that stinking hold for weeks now. This is an important moment, and

I'm not going to miss it."

Luke nodded. It was a big moment. Today, Harry Goodsir, the assistant surgeon on the *Erebus*, was going to bring out his daguerreotype, a wonderful new invention that could make pictures that looked as real as life.

The young men watched now as Goodsir and two other men wrestled the equipment off the ship's boat onto the shore. They began to set up a small tent and the camera—a large wooden box mounted on a tripod. When the camera was finally in place, Mr. Goodsir pointed it toward the two ships. Luke watched as the tall young Scotsman busily fussed with various knobs and plates and covers and looked at his pocket watch. He frequently threw up his hands and disappeared into the tent. It seemed to take forever, and Luke could see some of the officers beginning to fidget impatiently. They were all clean-shaven and decked out in full dress uniform, complete with epaulettes and stick-up collars.

Finally the smiling doctor emerged from the tent with a picture of the two anchored ships. He showed it to the group of men, and there were shouts of disbelief and approval. Then Goodsir waved, and the officers began to gather for a group portrait.

Below the railing, the *Terror*'s boat was getting ready to push off.

"If you two are coming to shore, make it quick," called up one of the sailors. "We're leaving now."

"This is it," Luke said to John. "They're going to take the group portrait. Let's go."

John nodded as they made their way over to the ship's ladder.

"All of England will see this picture," he said with a smile. "We'll be famous. Soon we'll be looking out over the Pacific Ocean, heroes, every one of us."

"Well, let's hurry then, or else we'll miss it."

Suddenly Luke was pulled to a stop. John was staring at him with a puzzled look on his face.

"What about that last load of coal?" he said. "We

Franklin's expedition was one of the first to carry a camera to the Arctic. Assistant surgeon Harry Goodsir once posed for his own picture.

must get it on board before the supply ship leaves today."

John had stepped away from him and was now standing very erect. He pulled his pipe out of his pocket and lit it. Then he took a few puffs and gazed at Luke sternly. With long wisps of lank brown hair hanging over his eyes, he looked almost comical, but Luke didn't feel like laughing.

"What are you talking about? The *Barretto Junior* doesn't leave for several days. Besides, she's loading the *Erebus* now. We won't begin to take on our fuel until tomorrow."

"As chief stoker I believe I give the orders," John said coldly, and there was an odd look in his eyes that made Luke's neck prickle. "The coal must be loaded now." Then, his body rigid with anger, John slowly crushed his clay pipe stem between his teeth, biting his lip in the process. A thin trickle of blood slowly dripped down his lower lip.

The squawk of a gull shattered the air over their heads, startling them both. John's face suddenly crumpled, and his eyes clouded over. He looked down and stared at his feet for a long time. Then he dropped the still-burning pipe bowl onto the deck.

"I don't feel very well," he murmured. "I think I'll go back to bed. It's just a picture, after all. It doesn't matter." He turned and began to shuffle back to the hatchway. Luke followed quickly, his face full of worry.

What was happening to his friend? What was going on?

All week long, Luke helped unload coal into the *Terror* from the *Barretto Junior*. The fuel for the steam engines and boilers took up much of the space below decks, and the ship was now very crowded. John had been well enough to supervise for a

Right: As Luke and John watch from the ship, Franklin and his officers arrange themselves for their portrait.

few days, but now he was back in sick bay. Nothing had been said about the episode on deck.

With the supply loading finally finished and their departure from Greenland imminent, Luke was enjoying his last day on firm land. Sir John encouraged all the crew members to wander about and collect specimens, so Luke had been out all morning gathering plants and shells and rocks. He had found some curious mosses and a flower that looked like a pin cushion, which he wanted to show John.

His friend looked better today. He was sitting at a small table, writing furiously.

"What are you doing?" asked Luke, peering over John's shoulder.

"I'm writing to my father. The supply ship is leaving tomorrow and this is our last chance to write. Everybody's sending letters home. Just think, the next letters we write will be mailed from a Russian sea port on the other side of the continent." John smiled broadly. "After that we'll be going home, to double pay, I'll wager."

"Fine by me," said Luke.

John looked at him hard. "Why don't I write a letter to your aunt and uncle for you? You can tell me what to say and I'll write it down. Then maybe we can get back to our reading lessons."

Luke smiled gratefully. Could this be the same man who had behaved so oddly just a few days ago? Then he noticed the spot where John had bitten his lip. The sore wasn't healing too well. It looked ugly and raw.

"After all," John went on. "It's only fair. You've been bringing me my meals. It's the least I can do in return. We'll look after each other, what do you say?" He started to

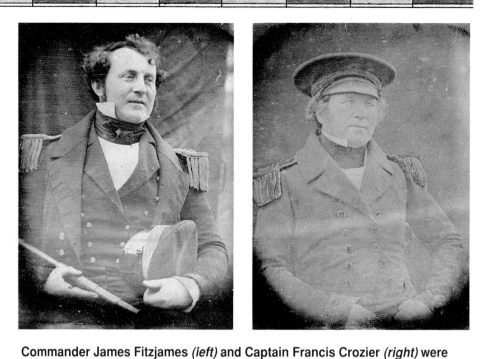

Commander James Fitzjames *(left)* and Captain Francis Crozier *(right)* were both experienced navy men. They looked after the daily operations on board the *Erebus* and the *Terror*.

This dip circle helped Franklin's crews distinguish the geographic North Pole from the North Magnetic Pole.

chuckle, but his laughter turned into a gasping fit of coughing.

The door to sick bay opened, and Surgeon Peddie walked in accompanied by Captain Crozier.

"Still coughing?" the doctor asked as he beckoned John over to the bed so he could examine him.

"Not too much, sir."

The doctor began to press John's stomach. "Any stomach pain?" he asked.

"None at all, sir," John said stiffly, but Luke could see the beads of perspiration that had broken out on his forehead.

"Well, seaman," the doctor announced briskly, "I'm afraid it would be best to send you home. The *Barretto Junior* is turning back in the morning." He nodded toward the men in the other beds. "You and four others will be sailing with her."

"But, sir," John protested, sitting bolt upright. He turned to Captain Crozier. "You can't do that. I'm well, truly!"

Captain Crozier frowned. "Mr. Peddie says you've shown almost no sign of improvement. How will you manage to get through an Arctic winter? The British Admiralty can't afford to support a man who can't perform his duties, you know."

"But I have been working, sir," John said. "I've been in the engine room every day. Ask Smith here."

Captain Crozier raised his eyebrows and turned to Luke. "Well?"

Luke swallowed and looked at John. He could see the pleading in his friend's eyes. He knew how much this voyage meant to him.

"Yes, sir, it's true," he said at last. "Mr. Torrington has worked every day. He's getting stronger by the hour."

"I only come back to sick bay for the good meals, sir," John laughed, and flashed the captain his broadest smile.

"Captain, I don't think—" Mr. Peddie began, but Captain Crozier was chuckling.

"Very well," he said. "You know what lies ahead. Besides, the local people have said that this summer is much milder and earlier than usual. If all goes to plan, Sir John thinks we may well get through the passage this season." Then he turned and left the room.

The doctor slowly turned to follow. At the door, he hesitated for a moment. Then he beckoned to Luke, who joined him in the doorway.

"By the way," the surgeon said in a low voice. "A few of the other sick men have been showing some odd symptoms. Not physical so much as..." He looked at Luke, and his eyes narrowed. "You haven't noticed any signs of...unusual behavior in your friend, have you?"

Luke looked back into the room at John, and their eyes held for just an instant.

"No, sir," Luke said to the doctor. "Nothing unusual. Nothing at all."

The *Erebus* and *Terror* were last seen by whaling ships off the Greenland coast in July 1845.

CHAPTER FOUR

WINTER CAMP
Beechey Island, late September 1845

Luke took several big gulps of fresh cold air and paused for a few minutes before going down the hatch. By now, the stench below deck was hard to take. The soot and grease from the lamps and candle flames coated the men's skin, clothing and hair. Most of the sailors smoked pipes, which added to the smell, and many of the men had stopped washing altogether, finding that a layer of dirt and grease on their bodies helped keep out the increasing cold as winter approached.

Luke gazed around him. They were anchored in a small protected bay just off Beechey Island. They had passed the island several weeks earlier on their search for the Passage. Then their way

For Franklin's men, who had no way to communicate with the rest of the world, the windswept shores of Beechey Island must have seemed the loneliest place on earth.

had been blocked by ice, and now with the sailing season rapidly coming to a close, they had been forced to come back here to spend the winter. Luke knew they might be ice-bound for as long as ten months.

They would not complete the passage this first year.

Across the bay, the rugged dark-gray cliffs of North Devon rose almost straight out of the water like the walls of a fortress. Behind the two ships lay Beechey Island, its gravel slopes gently rising up to a high, flat plain.

Luke listened. Except for the sounds of the men on the shore setting up the winter camp, it was very quiet here. Few birds, plants, or, thankfully, insects. He still had scars from the mosquitoes on Disco Island, which had left his neck raw.

The last three months had been a blur. There had been periods of intense boredom, like the week they spent in Baffin Bay waiting for the ice to clear. But then they had at last been able to cross the bay into Lancaster Sound. Luke would never forget the honking of the snow geese and screams of the gulls echoing off the sheer cliffs. And then they had entered a bleak stretch of smaller islands and channels, like a maze that you could never find your way out of. After a while, every icy path began to look the same.

They had seen a whaling ship at the end of July, when they spent several days moored to a drifting iceberg, but since then there had been no contact with the outside world. But already they had followed hundreds of miles of unexplored coast. They had changed the map of the world forever, just as John had promised they would.

John.

Luke went below and took a deep breath before going into sick bay. Every day it became more difficult to visit his friend, who was getting weaker and weaker. The medicines weren't helping; neither was the rest or good food. John only got out of bed now for his daily walks around the deck, which the doctor insisted on.

John was lying on his back, a bowl of tinned meat and potatoes propped on his chest.

"Here," he said when he saw Luke. "I can't eat it."

"Again?" Luke took the bowl from his friend.

"No. I don't want it. You can have it."

Luke shrugged and began to eat John's meal. It tasted delicious, but he couldn't help feeling guilty. This was the fourth day in a row that he had finished John's food for him, because John was still pretending to the doctors that he was eating well.

"Good, is it?" John asked. He looked almost pained at watching his friend eat with such gusto.

Luke shoveled a huge spoonful of meat into his mouth. "The rest of us are still eating salted fish," he said with his mouth full. "Some of the men were boasting about all the local birds they would shoot, but it's hardly made a difference. The best meat goes to the officers, anyway."

John nodded. "You need to bring down a bear or a caribou. Something bigger." He sighed deeply. "If I could just get off this ship."

Luke scraped the side of the bowl clean and put it down. "One

Some of Franklin's sailors tried to add to their rations of salt fish by shooting seabirds *(top)*. Whaling ships *(above)* hunted not for whale meat but for blubber which was made into oil and used to light lamps in England.

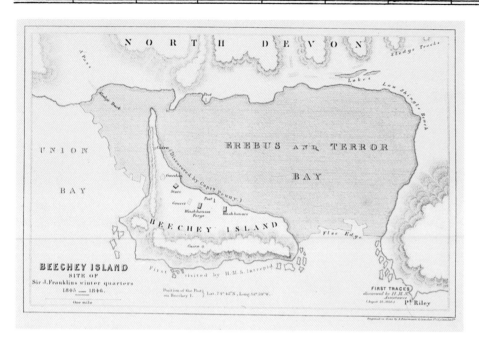

This map of Beechey Island was made by searchers who arrived there in 1852.

happens if the ice doesn't break up in the spring? You said yourself it can happen." Luke's voice began to rise.

"Why are you saying these things?" John was practically shouting. "We will find the passage before this winter. All of England awaits our return."

Luke stared at his friend. "But...we're anchored off Beechey Island for the winter. We'll be here until next spring. The captain has already said we won't be—"

John grabbed Luke's wrist. His grip was surprisingly fierce, and he spoke through gritted teeth.

"I know you're trying to keep things from me. I can't trust you anymore. I must find a way to talk to Sir John myself."

Luke was silent. He was too scared to say anything. Talk to Sir John? What could his friend mean?

More and more, he wished that John had gone back to England on the *Barretto Junior*.

of the men on the ship says the Eskimos in the north live off the meat they catch all the time. They use harpoons and hooks carved out of bone to catch fish and seals. Why can't we do that?"

John frowned and picked at the edge of his blanket. Luke noticed how pale and thin his hands were. "We could, I suppose, but why would we want to? We have thousands of pounds of tinned food on board."

"But what happens if our food runs out? What

When the weather turned cold, crewmen attempted to break a path through the ice for the ships.

The next morning, Luke helped to row the ship's boat over to the island camp. The bay was calm, and there was a glassy sheet of ice on the water that crunched gently as the prow of the boat broke it apart.

Soon the ships would be permanently locked in ice for the winter. There was much to be done before then. Already the weather was turning colder, and the hours of sunlight became fewer each day.

On the island, men were constructing a carpenter's shop, a large storehouse and a small canvas-covered wood-frame structure to house the forge and anvil. Tents were erected, as well as a number of observation platforms for surveying and lookouts. Beside a small stream, fed by the still-melting snow higher up on the island, stood a row of metal tubs to serve as a washing area for the crews.

The sound of gunshots came from the steep cliffs to the west. Luke followed the sound to the shooting gallery that had been set up farther down the beach.

By early fall the ice over the Arctic seas was too thick to break through. Franklin chose to spend the first winter of the expedition in a sheltered harbor off Beechey Island.

There William Braine, one of the royal marines from the *Erebus*, was practicing his marksmanship, aiming at a far-off pile of discarded tin cans.

"Want to try a shot, boy?" he asked when he noticed Luke.

"Yes, sir. Thank you." Luke stepped into the stone circle and watched carefully while Braine stuffed gunpowder and a bullet down the muzzle and handed him the gun. Luke hefted the shotgun to his shoulder, aimed and fired. He hit a tin can, and it popped into the air at the impact.

"You're not a bad shot, lad," said Braine, eyeing Luke keenly. "A polar bear was sighted near the camp this morning, and a group of us are going out to see if we can find it. I could use someone to help me carry my gear. Want to come along?"

ICE-BOUND IN THE ARCTIC

Once a safe harbor was found, the sailors worked quickly to prepare the ships for the Arctic winter. They knew that they could be ice-bound for ten months.

1) Sailors built a wall of snow blocks around the ship to add an extra layer of insulation.

2) All heavy supplies were taken off the ship so that it would be light enough to bob free of moving ice instead of being crushed between giant slabs of it.

3) A huge canvas tent was erected over the deck so that the sailors would have a place to exercise.

4) A hunting party heads off in search of fresh meat.

The *Erebus* carried a steam locomotive engine attached to a propellor. This powerful engine was meant to drive the ship through ice-blocked seas.

④

ater that afternoon, Luke trudged out of camp with a group of men from the *Erebus*. Among them were two young brothers, Thomas and John Hartnell, whom Luke had met a few days before. The sky was overcast, as usual. Over each shoulder was slung a rifle and a canvas bag filled with ammunition, food, knives and extra clothing.

"Normally I carry my own things," Braine explained. "But I've been in sick bay for much of the past week. Stomach cramps made me lose my appetite, but it's nothing serious. I'll be back to my old self in a day or two."

Luke glanced at the older sailor. For the first time he noticed the sheen of sweat on the tall man's wide brow, and how Braine's white skin stood out against his curly black beard and the red kerchief that he wore around his neck.

"Poor old John has been in and out of sick bay too," said Thomas Hartnell, glancing anxiously at his younger brother who walked behind them. "But all this fresh air and exercise is bound to do him good."

The small party headed across the narrow spit of land that joined Beechey Island to North Devon. Luke felt a prickle of anticipation in his stomach that he knew was both excitement and fear. Other men had seen as many as five polar bears at a time on Devon. He was sick to death of hearing how magnificent and powerful they were. For a long time now he had wanted to see one of these beasts for himself. Maybe this would be his chance.

The men wandered for over two hours. Luke hoped they wouldn't

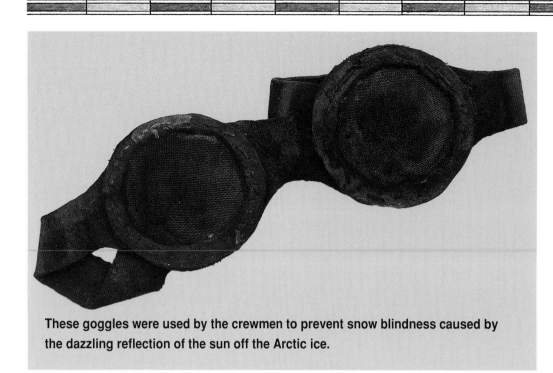

These goggles were used by the crewmen to prevent snow blindness caused by the dazzling reflection of the sun off the Arctic ice.

their guns, he noticed the bear's paws for the first time. They were the size of a man's head. Luke thought about the crushing power of those paws, and his mouth went dry.

Beside him, Braine was aiming carefully.

"Let me take him," the marine said, and as Luke watched, Braine fired.

The shot hit the bear, but to Luke's astonishment, it seemed to have no effect. The huge bear simply dropped to its legs and kept moving forward. He was coming toward them.

Braine reloaded quickly, and Luke could see that his hands were trembling. The marine aimed and shot again. A shower of ice exploded in front of the bear's head. It stopped in its tracks, but then kept coming.

The bear started to run toward them.

The other four men raised their guns now, but Luke was the fastest. Sighting along his rifle, he aimed and fired. The acrid smell of gunpowder filled his nostrils, and he closed his eyes against the smoke.

When he opened his eyes, Braine was clapping him on the shoulder, and the other men were running toward the bear that lay slumped on the ground, looking more like a hummock of snow than a man-eating beast.

"Well, congratulations, lad," Braine said heartily. "You've done a good job. We'll have fresh meat to eat for awhile, and you'll have something to talk about when you get home."

Luke smiled. He felt happy for the first time in weeks.

have to go too much farther. His woolen shirt was plastered against his skin with sweat, and it made him feel clammy and cold. He was also starting to feel very lost, almost dizzy. He would find himself tripping over a rock that he thought was miles away. Once the camp and the snow-streaked cliffs were out of sight, one hill looked much like the next. Sometimes it seemed as though the gray land and sky blended into one.

Besides, he could see that Braine was tiring. His breathing was raspy, and twice now he had stumbled for no reason.

Then, suddenly, there it was, about one hundred yards ahead of them. Luke wouldn't even have noticed it loping along if the bear hadn't stopped and raised its powerful body up on its hind legs to test the breeze for scent. Its huge forelegs hung straight down as if it stood at attention.

Luke was surprised that he didn't feel scared. The animal didn't look mean or threatening—just very, very big. As Luke and the other men raised

Right: Luke shoots a polar bear. Sailors without guns had to rely on their hands and their wits to repel bears *(above).*

DEATH IN THE ARCTIC

Beechey Island, January 1, 1846

The crew of the *Terror* collect snow for building blocks. Arctic temperatures can drop to -40°F (-40°C) so this was freezing work for the sailors in their thin wool clothing.

"**Y**ou shove me again, boy, and I'll drag you off this ship by your ear and nail you to the ground for bear bait."

Luke looked up into the angry eyes of the sailor he had stumbled against, but the man was so muffled up against the cold that Luke couldn't even tell who it was.

"Sorry," he muttered through his scarf, but nobody heard him. The men were already on the march again. Nobody spoke.

It's like a funeral procession, he thought.

Luke folded his arms across his chest for warmth.

Then he picked up his heavy feet and trudged on. His eyebrows and scarf were crusty with ice and his hands ached horribly. Yesterday he had grabbed hold of a frozen iron railing and even through his gloves the skin on his palms had burned and peeled away from the extreme cold. Above him, the canvas awning that had been spread over the upper deck snapped in the wind like gunshots. The awning provided little actual protection from the fierce winter gales—powdery snow worked its way through every crack and seam, so that the deck was always covered with a thick white layer.

Luke bent his head down and fixed his gaze on the feet of the man in front of him. He and about forty others paced slowly up and down the port side of the ship in rows of two or three, wrapped in their bulky winter clothing. On the starboard side stood an officer shielding a single candle that was the only light in the Arctic gloom.

It was just one-thirty in the afternoon.

They had been wintering on Beechey Island for over three months now, but to Luke it was starting to seem like a lifetime. The bustling autumn activity of setting up the camp, the hunting parties and exploring, the slippery games of rounders and blind man's bluff on the ice had ended. Now the sailors followed a numbing routine from the moment they were called by whistle to a breakfast of oatmeal and biscuits at seven-thirty in the morning to the tedious exercise marches and endless inspections and church services to the daily rations of lemon juice that they were all forced to take to guard against scurvy. And all this in the cramped, frigid quarters of the ship, under a sky that, since the first week in November, had been dark or murky twenty-four hours a day. The darkness was suffocating, as if it were burying them alive.

These days Luke often ached with homesickness. Many nights he would lie awake, shivering in his canvas coat and boots, and suddenly find tears streaming down his

During the bitter months of winter the only natural light in the Arctic is the glow of the aurora borealis or northern lights *(inset)*. Candles on Arctic ships were sometimes rationed to an inch a day.

face. He knew he wasn't alone. Even some of the most experienced seamen had broken down and wept in despair.

The polar bear hunt seemed like a dim memory now. Luke hadn't seen William Braine since that day. One of

Sir John Franklin died on June 11, 1847, but even today no one knows exactly how he died or where his body lies.

Braine's shipmates said the marine private had taken ill again, and had been back in sick bay on the *Erebus* for several weeks.

In fact, a number of the men were sick. Some suffered from frostbite. During one of his visits to see John, Luke had actually seen Surgeon Peddie amputate two of a man's fingers. And many of the men had lost weight. Even though Luke was still eating more than his share of tinned food, he, too, had found his appetite dulling.

But other sailors, like John, were weakening rapidly from an ailment that none of the doctors could explain.

Ships bound for the Arctic often carried theatrical costumes so that the men could entertain themselves with plays. These sailors are performing a historical drama.

Christmas had finally brought a bit of relief from the dull routine. Christmas dinner had been spectacular. The officers had mingled with the crew, and they had all celebrated into the night, drinking generous toasts to everyone from Queen Victoria and Lady Franklin right down to the ship's pet dog. On Christmas Eve, Sir John had come over to the *Terror* to speak to the men and visit the sick bay. Luke had watched the bear-like captain as he stood surrounded by his small group of officers, his hand resting gently on John Torrington's shoulder. Luke remembered being surprised at seeing Sir John without his hat on, his head almost bald as he leaned over to listen to the young sailor's whispers.

As the captain spoke to the sick man, Luke could see that his friend's breathing became more even. He couldn't hear what Sir John was saying, but the calming effect of his words was obvious.

When he went below deck after exercise period, Luke barely noticed the smell of baking bread and the rest of the dinner that was being prepared for a special New Year's feast. In the library, a group of men busily rehearsed for the play that they would be putting on that evening. A few of the officers laughed uproariously as they tried to squeeze the sailor who would be playing the heroine into a corset. Two empty bottles of wine stood on the table beside them.

"Going to visit the sick bay, lad?" asked one of the officers when he noticed Luke. "Want to take your book?" The laughter stopped, and the library suddenly became quiet. The officer picked up the book and held it out. It was *The Vicar of Wakefield*—the book that Luke had been learning to read for the past two months.

But Luke shook his head. He knew that John wouldn't be able to help him with his reading today.

In sick bay, John lay on his back with his eyes closed. Luke winced when he saw the leather straps that bound his friend to the bed. But he knew they were necessary. The night before, when Luke had offered to try to read to him, John had suddenly had a fit, screaming that Luke had stolen his journal, that he was trying to take all the glory for himself. He had actually tried to attack Luke, and Luke would never forget the feel of his friend's cold fingers around his neck, as John pathetically tried to shake him.

John didn't look as if he could attack anybody now. Luke walked over to the bed and gazed down at John's thin arms pinned helplessly under his binds. He looked over at Surgeon Peddie with a questioning glance, and the doctor understood and nodded.

As Luke unbuckled the leather straps, John's eyes opened. He stared right at Luke, and his dark-brown eyes were as clear and calm as Luke had ever seen them.

"You know, mate," John whispered. "I just wanted to be a part of something important. Something that people would remember and talk about..." Then his whole body trembled briefly, his eyes closed, and he was suddenly still.

Luke stared down at his friend's empty face. He scarcely felt the doctor's hands on his shoulders, turning him around and gently guiding him out of the room.

In the morning, from the upper deck, Luke could hear the sounds of the carpenter and his mate who were constructing John's coffin. Captain Crozier sent six men ashore to dig a grave, and even from the ship, Luke could hear their grunts of effort and the echoes of the pickaxes hacking at the frozen ground.

Luke went down to sick bay, where Surgeon Peddie was preparing the body for burial. After John's body was washed and clothed, cotton strips were torn from a sheet and used to bind the body to make it easier to lift into the coffin. As Luke watched, the doctor folded John's blue and white kerchief, wrapped it under the dead sailor's chin and tied it tightly at the top of his head.

Luke turned away. He didn't want to watch anymore. But he felt he had to do something.

Walking back through the mess hall, he noticed a barrel filled with empty tin cans. He took a tin from the pile and held it in his hand.

"Potatoes," he said, and almost smiled.

Luke sat down at the table and cut the ends off the tin. Then he split the side seam and carefully flattened the sheet of metal. He wiped the inner surface clean, and then painted it with blue paint. Then he slowly cut the piece of metal into the rough shape of a heart. When he was finished, he placed the heart near the galley stove so that the heat would dry the paint quickly.

With a small brush, he carefully painted fine guide lines across the heart, so the inscription would be perfectly straight. Then, holding his hand as steadily as he could, he painted on a message, slowly copying the letter shapes from a book: JOHN TORRINGTON DIED JANUARY 1ST 1846 AGED 20 YEARS.

He decorated the heart with a few flourishes and leaf shapes, and it was done.

By the following day, the preparations for the burial were nearly complete. Luke went up to the upper deck where the coffin was waiting. Then he handed the heart plaque to the carpenter, who took it without a word and nailed it to the lid of the coffin.

Our first view of John Torrington's coffin plate. We were touched by the care that had obviously been taken in making it.

It only took Luke and William Johnson to carry John's wasted body from the sick bay up to the coffin. They carefully laid the body on a thin layer of wood-chips that the carpenter had sprinkled in the bottom. The lid was quickly nailed in place.

It was time to bury John Torrington.

Luke, William and two other men carried the coffin to the starboard side of the ship, then lowered it down on ropes to the ice and snow below. There the coffin was swung onto a sledge, draped with a flag and lashed firmly in place.

A light snow began to fall. Two men attached har-nesses to the sledge and started hauling it toward the island. The ice was very uneven, and it took several men to help the sledge across the bumpy parts. All the

Top: Luke watches as John is buried. To reach the grave, the sailors had to strap the coffin to a sledge and haul it over hills of ice *(above)*.

men from the *Erebus* joined the march, and by the time they reached the sloping snow-covered gravel of Beechey Island, over one hundred sailors had gathered, including Sir John Franklin. Even William Braine was there, leaning heavily on the arms of two companions. When Luke waved to him, the gaunt, hollow-eyed man seemed not to know him.

Luke knew that only John Hartnell, from the *Erebus*, was missing. He was the only man too sick to make it off the ship. But Hartnell's older brother, Thomas, was in the crowd of sailors. Luke noticed how Thomas refused to look at the coffin. When Sir John read aloud a passage from the Bible by lamplight, the white pages rippling in the wind, Thomas Hartnell was the only one who wept.

Five days later, they buried John Hartnell. To Luke, it almost felt as if he were reliving his friend's funeral. From the deck of the *Terror* he heard the same sounds of men digging the grave. Later, he trudged with the rest of the crew behind the sledge. Once again the sledge jerked and scraped awkwardly over the uneven, crusty ice, but even so, Luke had to struggle to keep up. His legs were heavy, like stone, and his whole body felt weak, as if his blood were draining out of him through his feet.

I have to start eating more, he thought to himself. I have to keep up my strength. After all, they still had to survive several months of winter. He had heard some of the officers say that February and March were the worst, although he couldn't imagine how that could be possible.

At the graveside, he stood near the back of the crowd as Thomas Hartnell and the other men from the *Erebus* lowered the coffin into the ground.

Behind Luke stood John Peddie and Stephen Stanley, the surgeon of the *Erebus*.

"Mr. Goodsir and I did an autopsy of the body," Stanley said to his colleague in a low voice. "Two deaths in four days, less than a year after leaving England. The commander agreed that it was important we learn the cause."

Luke no longer heard the voice of Sir John reading from the Bible. An autopsy? Had they discovered why Hartnell died? Could it have been the same thing that had killed John Torrington? Could there finally be an explanation for his friend's slow, agonizing death, his odd behavior? Luke listened harder to the conversation of the surgeons.

"And?" asked Peddie.

"We found some small, hardened lumps in the lung tissue."

The *Terror*'s surgeon gave a sad sigh. "Thank God. With the men's symptoms, I was beginning to wonder— "

"No need to wonder further. There's no doubt."

The two men began to make their way toward the group of officers who were starting to walk past the grave, but Luke didn't follow them.

He had watched both his parents die of tuberculosis. Even back in England the deadly disease was common. They, too, had suffered from terrible weakness, the painful, forced breathing, the wracking cough.

Luke frowned. He couldn't remember them behaving the way John had—the confusion, the fits, the look of madness. Still, they had died a long time ago. He could have forgotten.

Later that afternoon, the men were back on the *Terror*. A gale had blown in, and everyone was below decks whiling away the time until dinner. The excitement of Christmas and New Year had worn off. The men's faces looked ghostly and drawn in the lamplight. Nobody spoke.

As Luke wandered through the library, one of the officers approached him and handed him a book. It was *The Vicar of Wakefield*.

"I could help you read this, lad," said the man. "Now that your friend's gone—"

This dramatic painting shows the crew of the *Terror* preparing the ship for its first winter at Beechey Island. By spring, three of the expedition's sailors were dead.

Luke looked up, but for some reason the officer's kind face made him confused and angry. Who was this man, and why was he talking to him this way? Was he making fun of him? Something in Luke flared, and he heard himself shout and felt his hands reach out and close tightly around the man's neck. Suddenly he was squeezing as hard as he could, and he didn't know why.

Then strong arms came around him from behind and

pulled him away.

The next thing he knew, the officer was sitting in a chair, rubbing his neck. A thin line of blood bubbled up where Luke's nails had scratched him.

The officer stared at Luke with fury, and fear.

"He tried to kill me," he said, his voice raspy. "I want the boy put in leg irons immediately. He's a threat to —"

Two officers had Luke pinned to the wall now, but there was no need. His body had gone limp, and he was panting for breath.

"Take it easy," one of them said to the angry officer.

"The lad's friend is dead. It's the grief talking. He's not himself, isn't that right, lad? You're grieving for Petty Officer Torrington." The man turned to the young stoker anxiously.

Luke sat on the floor, his legs drawn stiffly up to his chest. He stared blankly at the sea of uniforms around him, the brass buttons glinting in the smoky lamplight, the worried stares of waxy, bleached faces.

Even from where he sat he could hear the Arctic winds howling around the ice-bound ship. He felt heavy inside—John was gone. And he was beginning to doubt that he would ever see the shores of England again.

CHAPTER SIX

UNRAVELING THE MYSTERY

Beechey Island, August 1984

lthough I was anxious to begin excavating the graves of the three men who had died on Franklin's expedition during the early months of 1846, we had to set up camp first.

Over the next two hours we put up our large cooking tent and organized our field equipment and food supplies. We set up our sleeping tents some distance up the beach, so that the food was between us and the bay. This was a necessary precaution considering

that Beechey Island lies along a polar bear migration route. Polar bears coming out of the bay to snoop around our camp would discover our food a long way from us. We also put up an electrical alarm fence around the sleeping tents to warn us if a bear visited us while we were asleep. And we had rifles as a final protection against these powerful, inquisitive animals.

After our own tents were assembled, we put up an antenna and connected our radio. We would

Above: Team members set up camp. We pitched the tents where food was stored far from our sleeping tents to keep hungry polar bears away from us, but this curious bear *(inset)* came close enough to be photographed.

be in contact twice a day with the Canadian government base at Resolute Bay. Both the success and safety of our project depended on the radio, our only link with the outside world.

How different this was, I thought, from Franklin's situation. No radio, no outside contact. Nobody knew where in the vast Arctic the ships were. No wonder it took so long to find any trace of the expedition.

There was a small stream running beside our camp — the same stream Franklin and his men had used 140 years earlier — and we scooped cold water from it for washing and cooking. Our food consisted of pasta, oatmeal, tinned and freeze-dried food, and a small amount of fresh fruit and vegetables.

The warm rooms, soft beds and good food of the government facilities in Resolute Bay seemed far away as we all zipped into our sleeping bags at the end of our first day. The numbing cold of the permafrost was just a few inches beneath our sleeping pads.

Within the next few days we would dig down into even colder layers of that permafrost in our search for the causes of the Franklin disaster.

We were planning to dig up the body of John Torrington first. We knew that Torrington had died early in the expedition, and we wanted to find out why. It had taken an enormous amount of preparation to secure all the necessary permits

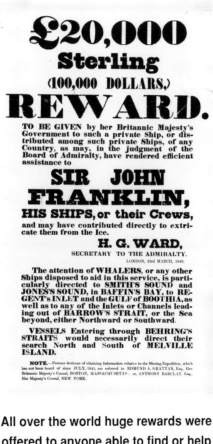

All over the world huge rewards were offered to anyone able to find or help Franklin and his men.

from the authorities, as well as attempting to contact any known relatives of the dead man. Now, at last, we had the permission we needed to open the grave and examine the body, and none of us took the responsibility lightly. We only hoped that our work would be justified — that the knowledge we gained might then help explain the misery and death that had followed for the others. And we hoped above all that we might bring some light to a moment of history that had, for so long, been shrouded in mystery.

We weren't, of course, the first to search for Franklin and to try to unravel the mystery of the lost expedition. When the *Erebus* and the *Terror* did not return, no one was worried for a long time. The expedition had enough supplies to last for three years, and experienced Arctic explorers knew how easily a passage could become blocked by ice, which could add several months to a journey. Sir John Franklin was too seasoned a commander, his ships too sturdy and well equipped for anything to go seriously wrong.

Besides, England had already sent over fifty expeditions to the Arctic and, though they had suffered great hardship and some deaths, someone had always returned.

But when Franklin was not heard from for three years, people in England started to get anxious. They were worried for his safety and the well-being of the crews, of course. But maybe even more than that, no one wanted to believe that something could have gone wrong. Everyone had heard about the gut-chilling Arctic cold and the forbidding icy landscape. They realized that a ship in trouble would probably be impossibly far from help. Yet people could simply not accept that the most well-supplied, well-planned and well-commanded expedition of all time might have met with disaster.

So for the next ten years, more than forty expeditions set out for the Arctic to search for Franklin. A huge reward was offered to anyone who could bring back any news of him.

Search parties began looking for Franklin in 1848, but it wasn't until 1850 that the three graves were discovered on the shore of tiny Beechey Island. Near the graves were stone rings where tents had been erected, the gravel foundations of a storehouse and carpenter's house, the remnants of a garden, a shooting gallery, several lookout platforms and a neat pile of over seven hundred empty tin cans — evidence that Sir John had spent many months at Beechey Island. The searchers looked hopefully for a message telling where the ships were planning to sail, but found none.

Why had three men died so early in the expedition? Where were Sir John and the other 125 men? And where were the *Erebus* and the *Terror*?

Over the next few years searchers began to look even harder. They set out from the search vessels in large sledging parties. They tied notes to hydrogen-filled balloons and released them, in the hopes that they would be carried by the wind to the missing sailors. They painted giant messages on the sides of cliffs, and left stone caches filled with food, hoping that the lost men would find them. They even trapped foxes and put collars on them which had messages attached, in case one of Franklin's crew shot them.

Still, nothing more was found, and the searchers sailed home where they were welcomed coolly by many disappointed relatives and friends of Franklin's crew. On January 20, 1854, a notice appeared in a London newspaper announcing that unless the lost explorers were found by March, they would be listed as having died in the service of Queen Victoria.

But then, on October 23, 1854, Dr. John Rae, an explorer who journeyed overland living like the Inuit, met natives far south of the other search areas. These Inuit had silver forks and spoons from the Franklin expedition, as well as one of Franklin's own medals. They told Rae that they had heard from other Inuit about forty white men walking south. The men were pulling the ships' lifeboats mounted on sledges, and had dragged them over King William Island until they dropped dead of starvation. Their ships, the Inuit had heard, had been crushed in the ice.

Dr. Rae hurried to England to report his sad news, but he was not able to answer all the questions asked of him. He had not actually visited the scenes described to him by the Inuit, and many people doubted the accuracy of his reports.

In 1857, Lady Jane Franklin hired Captain Francis Leopold M'Clintock to find out whether Rae's story was true. In 1859 on King William Island, M'Clintock met another group of Inuit who had many Franklin relics in their possession, including silver cutlery and buttons.

Right: In 1854 Dr. John Rae met Inuit who had heard of a group of white men trying to walk out of the Arctic. From them he bought a medal which had once belonged to Sir John Franklin *(below)*.

LADY JANE'S SEARCH

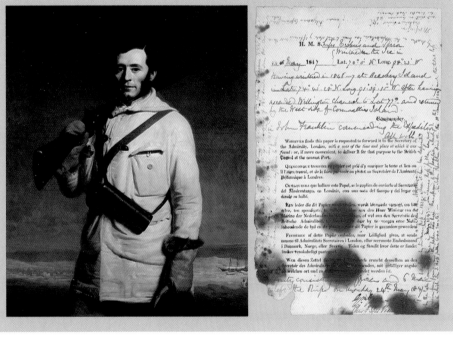

Lady Jane Franklin (above) never gave up hope that she would someday learn the fate of her lost husband. She asked the British government, the President of the United States and the Emperor of Russia for help in finding the missing men. This determination made her a heroine in Britain. In 1857 she hired Captain M'Clintock (right) to help in her search. His men discovered the cairn on King William Island (above right) that contained the only written record of what had happened to Franklin's crew (far right).

These people described finding a wrecked ship, and told of seeing Englishmen who "fell down and died as they walked."

Finally, on the island's southern coast, M'Clintock found the evidence everyone had been looking for. On a beach ridge, he came across a bleached white human skeleton dressed in the shreds of a steward's uniform lying face down in the gravel. Close by lay a small clothes brush and pocket comb.

And farther north was a rock cairn containing two notes written on a single piece of paper. The first note was dated May 28, 1847. It reported that the expedition had spent its first winter at Beechey Island and its second off the northwest coast of King William Island.

But around the margin of the paper was a second message. Written nearly a year later, it described how the *Erebus* and *Terror* had been trapped in ice off King William Island since September 12, 1846, and had been deserted on April 26, 1848, nearly three years after setting sail from England. Twenty-four men had died, including Sir John Franklin. The note added that the 105 survivors were planning to walk south in the hopes of reaching the Back River. They could then row up the inland river system to the nearest fur trade fort.

Clearly the attempt to reach safety by land was a desperate move after the ships had been trapped in the ice

for nineteen months, as their food supplies dwindled. The journey to that river was one that none of the men would complete. Final proof that their march was doomed to failure was found along the coast south of the cairn at a spot that was later to be known as the "Boat Place."

There M'Clintock came upon a lifeboat from one of Franklin's ships. The heavy boat was mounted on a sledge. Inside the boat, along with huge amounts of supplies that included everything from silk handkerchiefs, button polish, heavy cookstoves, and religious books to scented soap, curtain rods and toothbrushes, were two human skeletons. One appeared to have been disturbed by animals, but the other remained untouched, wrapped in cloth and fur, with feet tucked snugly into a pair of boots.

Propped against the side of the lifeboat were two loaded guns, as if ready to be shot at a polar bear or fired

into the air to catch the attention of rescuers. But for Franklin's men, the rescue had come eleven years too late. M'Clintock returned to England with news of his discoveries, and after that public interest in the Franklin mystery died down.

Still, the voyages of the dedicated explorers who searched for Franklin, many of whom also lost their lives in the Arctic, were not made in vain. Because of their efforts, much of the unknown North was explored and mapped. And, by the time I made my first trip to the Arctic in 1981, we did know a great deal about the fate of Franklin's men and just how desperate their last days had been.

I had examined the bones we had found on King William Island in 1981, and as I was looking closely at a thigh bone, my attention had been captured by something unexpected.

Many of the bones collected at Booth Point had

marks on them made by the teeth of animals like the Arctic fox, but three of the marks on this thigh bone looked different. Using a high-power hand lens, I closely examined the scratches. There was soon little doubt in my mind.

These were not tooth marks left by animals. They were knife-cut marks.

I remember slouching back in my chair as the significance of this discovery sank in. The awful possibility of cannibalism among Franklin's dying men was first mentioned by the Inuit in the 1850s, but these reports were greeted with stunned disbelief in Britain. Yet the thigh bone I held in my hand seemed to prove that cannibalism had taken place during the last dark days of the expedition.

My thoughts flashed back 136 years as I imagined Captain Crozier and Captain Fitzjames writing the famous note explaining that they were going to "start on tomorrow...for Back...River."

I pictured the survivors abandoning the familiarity of their ships in the still bitterly cold Arctic spring. Weak with hunger, but determined to return home, they dragged heavy sledges laden with boats full of unnecessary objects across the frozen wasteland toward a destination they would never reach. The icy winds would have cut through their thin woolen clothing as snow filled their cracked seamen's boots. The crewmen's feet and hands would have become so sore with frostbite that they could only hobble along, mile after frozen mile. Their courage must have flagged with each step. Some sailors probably gave up, turning back toward the ships. And as M'Clintock discovered, others simply died in their tracks.

How many, I wondered, became so desperate that they resorted to cannibalism? The tragic deaths of John Torrington, John Hartnell and William Braine seemed almost fortunate compared to the last terrible days of these sailors who, one by one, froze to death.

My disturbing discovery had only made me more anxious to solve the Franklin mystery. We knew when, and where, the expedition came to an end. But we did not yet know why.

Would John Torrington's body be well enough preserved to provide the final clue to what had happened in those last nightmarish months when the brave expedition went so wrong?

In 1848 Franklin's sailors made a desperate attempt to walk to safety. Starving and exhausted, they dragged their boats south until they could go no farther *(above)*. Eleven years later, M'Clintock's party made a grisly discovery at what came to be known as the "Boat Place" *(left)*.

CHAPTER SEVEN

FRANKLIN'S SAILORS LIVE AGAIN

Beechey Island, August 1984

It was like a scene from a horror movie, I thought to myself. In the gnawing Arctic cold, as the wind ripped around us and a massive black cloud rolled in over the site, our team hacked through five feet (1.5 metres) of cement-hard frozen earth. The air around the site was quiet, even solemn, as we sweated to expose the coffin. Not since the early years of Queen Victoria's reign had men dug at this site, and then it was to bury their shipmate, John Torrington.

Before we began our excavations, the frozen grave site had to be carefully staked out in a one-metre grid pattern with string and metal stakes. The criss-crossing of the strings in the grid was like placing a huge sheet of graph paper over the

Before we could begin to dig (above), we made a complete record of the appearance of each grave (top).

area. Every detail of the grave was mapped, measured, sketched and photographed so that when we finished, we could leave it exactly as it had been found.

To assist in the grave's reconstruction, we numbered each of the stones that covered the burial mound with water-soluble ink. Over the months after we left the site, rain, sleet and melting snow would eventually wash away these numbers.

It took two long and difficult days to chop through the frozen rock using picks and shovels. We took turns breaking up the permafrost one small chunk at a time. The broken pieces were then shoveled into a bucket and dumped on a large plastic sheet beside the grave.

At last research assistant Walt Kowal carefully

swept aside the remaining layer of ice and gravel.

"That's it. We've got it," he declared. Everyone was very quiet. We were all thinking about the huge responsibility of disturbing Torrington's cold sleep.

I hunched beside Walt in the grave. First, blue wool fabric came into view—a coffin covering, and then a gleaming dark blue-green plaque cut into a heart shape. The white lettering read, "JOHN TORRINGTON DIED JANUARY 1ST 1846 AGED 20 YEARS"

I ran my hand over the rough edges of the metal. Someone had carefully cut the heart from what may have been a tin can, and painstakingly painted it.

But we had to push on. I wanted the coffin to be exposed for as little time as possible to limit any damage that could be done by the weather and by thawing.

Slowly we removed the mahogany coffin lid, only to reveal a solid block of ice that would take hours to defrost. Through the frozen bubbles and cracks in the ice, I could see something, but the more closely I looked, the more blurry it became.

With warm water we melted the ice encasing the body of John Torrington. As it thawed, I could first make out Torrington's striped shirt, every mother-of-pearl button in place. Then his perfectly preserved toes poked through the ice.

Finally I peeled away the last covering—the blue

fabric that covered the sailor's face—and we all reeled back in surprise and awe.

"He's there, he's right there!" gasped Arne Carlson, one of the field assistants. Torrington's thin face, with his half-closed eyes gazing through light-brown lashes, had a peaceful expression.

"It's as if he's just unconscious," I whispered. There, perfectly preserved in the Arctic permafrost, was a sailor from the Franklin expedition dressed in his Victorian clothing. Wrapped round his chin and knotted

After 48 hours of digging, we reached John Torrington's coffin *(inset)*. Everyone stood back in awe when the face of the young sailor was revealed *(above)*.

tightly at the top of his head was a kerchief, and surrounding his head were many wood shavings. When the men of the HMS *Terror* were preparing Torrington for burial, they secured his body by tightly tying strips of cotton around his body at his elbows, hands, ankles and toes. Obviously, a great deal of care had been taken during the burial. Suddenly I felt tremendous sadness for this young man's passing. In many ways he looked as if he had just died, yet he had come from a world so different from our own.

As leading stoker on the *Terror*, Torrington's job had been to shovel heavy loads of coal into the ship's engine. I expected his hands to be covered with calluses, but they looked delicate and smooth.

"They're like you would expect a pianist's to be," I marveled. He must have been too sick to work for a long time before he died. Even through his clothing, he looked extremely thin.

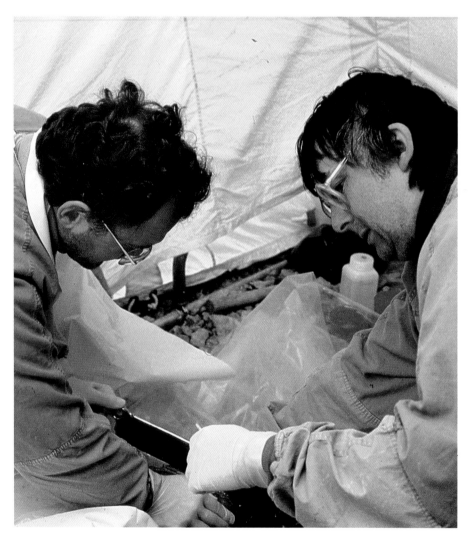

Dr. Roger Amy *(left)* and I perform an autopsy on one of the sailors. We hoped the results of our tests would tell us the cause of their deaths.

There was silence around the excavation site. Each one of us, I think, was imagining what this man's final days must have been like.

But why had he died? Only a medical autopsy would tell us.

During the next four hours, we examined the body and collected bone, hair and tissue samples for later analysis. After we were finished, we carefully laid

Torrington's reclothed body back in the coffin. The lid was replaced. Water, seeping naturally back into the grave, would soon freeze and seal it again.

Then the entire team gathered for a few moments of silence and prayer before assigning Torrington once again to the frozen depths, just as the crews of the *Erebus* and *Terror* would have done 138 years before. But while they paused for John Torrington on that bitter day in January 1846, none could have guessed what horror his death foretold. Their adventure was young, and the Northwest Passage, which had haunted men for over three hundred years, beckoned somewhere across the icy waters to the west.

Now I faced an important decision. Our time on Beechey Island was almost up, and each hour seemed to bring winter closer. Winds were colder, and temperatures regularly dipped below freezing. Before long the island would be covered in snow, and the tiny bay where Sir John Franklin's ships once lay at anchor would again fill with a crush of ice.

Should we leave before the weather grew any worse, perhaps trapping us on the island for days, or should we continue with our work, this time unearthing the frozen coffin of John Hartnell?

Something was bothering me about Hartnell's grave. It looked different from the other two, as if it had already been opened. I decided we'd have to investigate, even if it meant risking bad weather.

The excavation of Hartnell's grave proved to be even more difficult than that of John Torrington.

"Someone sure did a number on this grave," Walt said, pointing to a gaping hole in the coffin lid. It was clear that at some point following Hartnell's burial, someone had opened the coffin.

Again, the body was perfectly preserved. But when

One look at John Hartnell's coffin was enough to tell us that we were not the first to disturb his Arctic slumber.

The worsening weather at Beechey Island that summer brought an abrupt end to our work, and it was two years before I was able to return to the island to conduct autopsies on Hartnell and the third sailor, William Braine.

But by this time I had learned who had opened Hartnell's grave—searchers in 1852 who thought there might be a note inside, or some indication of what had happened to Franklin and the rest of the crews. They had been disappointed.

As before, we found the digging to be extremely difficult. Unearthing Hartnell's coffin required twenty-four hours of continual labor by four men. While they worked, I went to explore a food tin dump left by Franklin's men in 1846.

I knew that Sir John Franklin's expedition had been loaded full of food packed in tin cans — 8,000 of them.

(*continued on page 58*)

the area around the face was thawed, we were shocked by what we saw.

The sailor's lips had frozen into a snarl, and his partly exposed face, framed in ice, looked like a frightening, shimmering mask—the face of a sailor who had suffered a terrible death.

Even in July, when the sun shines for nearly 24 hours a day, it can seem like winter in the Arctic. This summer snowstorm took us by surprise and we had no place to go for shelter except back to our tents.

The cold which claimed the lives of many of their shipmates helped preserve John Hartnell *(right)* and two others so that they could complete the story of the lost expedition. This same cold froze the earth so hard that a man could only dig for twenty minutes before he was forced to stop *(top)*. We carefully thawed the ice around each coffin with warm water *(bottom left)*.

The delicate work on his coffin plate *(upper left)* did not prepare us for our first sight of William Braine's sea-toughened face *(above)*. The silverware found with the Inuit *(left)* would have been used by Braine's superior officers.

Above: Arctic clothing specialist Barbara Schweger examines clothing worn by Franklin's men. These cotton gloves *(right)* found at Beechey Island and leather boots *(above right)* from Starvation Cove were too thin to protect the men from the Arctic winter.

During most of the nineteenth century, tins were sealed shut with a mixture of lead and tin called solder. Could these tins have been a source of lead poisoning?

I spent the day carefully documenting what was left of the cans. With the assistance of archaeologist Eric Damkjar, I was able to examine closely the remains of about 150 of the cans. We collected ten samples for later

Tins discarded by Franklin's sailors still litter Beechey Island *(above and below)*. A lead and tin solder seam *(inset)*. Eating food from these tins would eventually prove fatal.

study and detailed analysis back in my laboratory in Edmonton.

I returned to camp just as Hartnell's coffin was about to be reopened. This time the event was made even more moving by the presence of Brian Spenceley, our photographer. Brian was John Hartnell's great-great nephew. When the coffin lid was opened, he was able to gaze into the eyes of a relative who had been dead for 140 years.

This time, as Hartnell's body slowly appeared through the melting ice, we could see that he wore a cap and that his head was resting on a small pillow. Soon we could see that his body, except his head, had been wrapped in a shroud, much like a cotton sheet. Beneath the shroud, Hartnell, like Torrington, looked very thin. Whatever his illness had been, it had robbed him of the will or ability to eat.

On this trip, the research team included two x-ray experts. X-rays of Hartnell and Braine would provide additional information about their lives and deaths. The first films, however, were confusing. None of John Hartnell's internal organs appeared to be in the right place. We had to wait until Hartnell's clothing was removed to find out why.

We soon discovered that the doctors on board the *Erebus* had performed an autopsy on him shortly after his death.

From examining the features of that first autopsy, Dr. Roger Amy, who was overseeing our study of Hartnell, was able to see what those doctors had determined to be Hartnell's cause of death: tuberculosis.

They would not likely have suspected any other cause.

B y the time I left Beechey Island that summer I had collected samples of frozen tissue, hair and bone from John Hartnell as well as the third sailor, William Braine.

The difficult, time-consuming work of examining and then carefully reburying each of these long-dead sailors had left all of us mentally and physically exhausted. But I knew the real work was just beginning. It would now take several months of study and analysis before we knew whether the samples that I carried in an insulated cooler would provide me with the final answers to the Franklin mystery.

Photographs and grids helped us to reconstruct the sailor's graves. It was important to leave them exactly as we'd found them.

In the meantime, I knew that I had already had a rare and humbling privilege in being able to gaze into the eyes of three men who had lived so long ago, and who had clearly suffered so much. No one will ever know how those men spent their last days, or what they had felt. But for those few brief hours during the Arctic summers of 1984 and 1986, they had lived again for me.

In early 1987 the test results were at last ready. Lab tests on bone and tissue samples from Torrington, Hartnell and Braine showed the same excessively high lead content as the Booth Point skeleton and the bones we had found in our 1982 investigation of the

Boat Place. And an analysis of the hair samples proved that these men had suffered from acute lead poisoning while they were on the Franklin expedition.

I was struck by the horrifying truth—lead had contributed to the declining health of the entire crews of the *Erebus* and the *Terror*. Not only did the sailors suffer from loss of appetite, weakness and other physical symptoms of lead poisoning, but the lead probably also affected their minds, making them behave strangely.

Many of them may have been unusually irritable, filled with unreal fears, incapable of clear thought and unable to make important decisions.

In some cases, like those of the three men buried on Beechey Island, the lead would prove fatal. Some of the autopsy results showed that Torrington, Hartnell and Braine all suffered from tuberculosis and possibly died from pneumonia. But it was lead, entering their bodies at high levels during the first months of the Franklin expedition, that poisoned and weakened the three men, allowing the other diseases to claim their lives.

I then carefully studied the tin can fragments that I had collected at Beechey Island. In Franklin's time, this new invention had allowed food to be preserved indefinitely, so that explorers could take with them supplies for long voyages. But the cans Franklin carried were seriously flawed.

I could see that the metal edges and seams of the cans were sealed on the inside with large pieces of solder made of melted lead and tin. In some cases there was so much solder that it had dripped and hardened like candle wax. While the can was full, lethal doses of lead from the solder would have dissolved into the food.

Our research also proved that the lead that poisoned the sailors could only have come from the canned foods—the composition of the lead in the bodies and in the solder was identical. How ironic it was, I thought, that the canned foods which should have allowed the men to survive for years in the Arctic were instead the cause of the early deaths of many sailors. It was not until the 1890s, long after the disaster, that the British government finally banned soldering on the inside of food tins.

The men aboard Franklin's mighty expedition expected to succeed, in part because they carried the tools and knowledge of the latest technology of Queen Victoria's time. And yet they died as a result of one of those new inventions. Lead poisoning was certainly not the only cause of the Franklin disaster. Once the supply of food ran out, starvation and scurvy claimed the last survivors. But it was the lead hidden in the food supply that slowly poisoned them all, playing an important role in the poor health and judgment that doomed the famous expedition.

When Sir John Franklin sailed from the River Thames in May 1845, an entire nation believed the honor of conquering the Northwest Passage was within his grasp. None could have guessed that inside the tins stored within the ship's hold there lurked a time bomb just as dangerous as the cruel Arctic winter.

The belief that British ways of dressing and eating were superior to all others was one of the reasons Franklin's men, and many others, froze and starved to death in the Arctic. These explorers are dressed for English spring weather. It was not until years after the Franklin tragedy that Europeans adopted native ways and donned warm fur clothing, used sleds pulled by dogs instead of by men, and ate raw meat to guard against scurvy.

Our team posed for a group portrait *(top)* before saying goodbye to the lonely graves *(above)*.

Exploring the frontiers of our world is one of the most exciting human quests. But it can also be the most dangerous, especially when exploration relies on untried technology. This fact was vividly demonstrated recently. In 1986, while the entire world watched in shock, one of the booster rockets of the space shuttle *Challenger* failed shortly after it left the ground, destroying the shuttle and killing all seven people on board.

Indeed, those explorers of space shared a bond with Sir John Franklin. Both used the most advanced technology of their time, and both suffered tragic losses as a result. In 1855, the year after the British government declared that Sir John Franklin and his brave crewmen had died in the service of Queen Victoria, one writer complained of the inhuman toll of Arctic research, arguing that their lives had been thrown away.

But Franklin, and those who joined his expedition, understood many of the risks involved in Arctic exploration. It wasn't enough for them to speculate about the last unknown shores on earth. Even though no sailor would actually use the dangerous Arctic passage as a route to the Far East, Franklin and his men wanted to chart those cold Arctic islands, to explore a land never before seen by Europeans, to be the first to find the Northwest Passage which had been sought after for more than three hundred years.

No one would take a ship all the way through the Northwest Passage until Norway's Roald Amundsen, conquered it in 1905. But Franklin's failure was, in one sense, a victory. For the searchers who followed his trail through the ice succeeded not only in opening up the great Canadian Arctic, but in challenging the last and most forbidding land on earth.

GLOSSARY

Able-bodied Seaman: An ordinary sailor on a ship.

Admiralty: The department in charge of the British navy.

amputate: To cut off a part from the body, such as a limb, because of injury or disease.

anthropologist : A person who studies anthropology, the scientific study of the human organism and human customs.

anvil: A heavy steel block where metal can be hammered.

archaeologist: Someone who studies archaeology, the scientific study of people from the past and their cultures.

armorer: The person who looks after the firearms aboard a ship.

autopsy: The examination of a corpse to determine the cause of death.

bowsprit: A large wooden rod projecting from the front of a ship.

cache: A secure place to store provisions.

cairn: A heap of stones piled up as a memorial or to mark a path.

cannibalism: The eating of human flesh by a human being.

Caucasian: A person who is a member of the white race.

daguerreotype: An early type of photograph produced on a silver or a silver-covered copper plate. Named after Louis Daguerre (1789-1851), the French painter and physicist who invented it.

decipher: To make out the meaning of a piece of writing.

draftsman: A person skilled in drawing plans and sketches.

epaulettes: Shoulder ornaments on a uniform or coat.

excavation: The action or process of digging something out to expose it to view.

forge: A workshop with a fireplace where metal objects are manufactured.

geographic North Pole: The most northerly point on the earth.

harpoon: A barbed spear with a rope attached used in hunting large fish or whales.

hatchway: A passage leading down to the area below the deck of a ship where the cargo is stored.

hydrogen: A colorless, tasteless, odorless, gaseous element, the lightest substance known.

Inuit: The native people who live in Canada's North and the Arctic. In the past they were called Eskimos.

mahogany: A reddish-brown wood from a tropical tree, often used to make furniture.

mess: The place on a ship where meals are eaten.

North Magnetic Pole: One of the two points around which the earth's magnetic field is arranged. This point shifts each year, but is always near the geographic North Pole. Metal compasses point to this pole instead of the geographic North Pole.

permafrost: A permanently frozen layer of ground below the surface in polar regions.

Petty officer: A naval officer chosen from among the ordinary sailors.

pneumonia: An inflammation of the lungs.

Queen Victoria: The queen of England from 1837 to 1901.

ration: The amount of food given to each sailor each day.

rounders: A game resembling baseball played with a bat and ball between two sides.

scurvy: A disease caused by lack of vitamin C.

shroud: A sheet-like garment used to wrap the dead.

sick bay: The area occupied by sick people aboard ship.

solder: A mixture of melted tin and lead used to join together metal surfaces.

soot: Fine pieces of black powder found in smoke.

steward: The member of a ship's crew responsible for distributing supplies.

stoker: Someone who feeds and tends the furnace of a steam engine.

tripod: A three-legged camera support.

tuberculosis: An infectious disease often found in the lungs.

THE SEARCH FOR THE NORTHWEST PASSAGE

1508
■ Explorer Sebastian Cabot thinks there might be a route north and west around the New World to Asia. He sails as far north as the Hudson Strait, but his crew, frightened by the sight of icebergs in July, force him to turn back.

1610-1611
■ Henry Hudson sails into a great body of water and believes he has reached the Pacific. After a winter in the ice, his crew mutinies and Hudson is forced into the ship's boat and left to drift. He is never seen again.

1615 & 1616
■ On his first *(dotted line)* and second *(solid line)* voyages in search of the Northwest Passage, William Baffin sails into the Arctic until he is stopped by ice. He concludes that there is no passage to the west to be found by sailing north and turns back.

1820
■ William Edward Parry makes amazing progress, sailing as far west as Melville Island before he is stopped by ice. Parry and his crewmen are the first Europeans to spend the winter locked in ice off an Arctic island.

1845-1848
■ The Franklin expedition spends its first winter at Beechey Island and the next two winters locked in ice off King William Island. The survivors abandon the ships and, dragging heavy sledges, attempt to walk south. Not one of them completes the journey.

1848-1859
■ The British send out over forty expeditions to find the missing ships, three of them paid for by Lady Franklin. During their searches, these ships explore previously unmapped areas of the Arctic and help to chart the route for a Northwest Passage.

1859
■ A search party led by Leopold M'Clintock discovers a cairn with a note inside explaining that the last of Franklin's men intend to march south to safety. M'Clintock proves that in their final march, the survivors walked across the last uncharted gap in the Northwest Passage.

1903-1906
■ Norwegian Roald Amundsen sails in search of the Northwest Passage in the little *Gjöa*. He and his crew spend two winters on King William Island living with and learning from the Inuit then travel on to make the first complete Northwest Passage by boat.

1984-1986
■ Anthropologist Owen Beattie and his field assistants search for solutions to the Franklin mystery. By examining the bodies of sailors preserved in the Arctic ice, Beattie discovers that lead poisoning from food tins played a role in the expedition's disastrous end.

RECOMMENDED FURTHER READING

Mystery in the Frozen Lands
by Martyn Godfrey 1988
(James Lorimer and Company, Canada)
In 1857, fourteen-year-old Peter Griffin sails to the Canadian Arctic with Captain M'Clintock aboard the *Fox* in search of Sir John Franklin.

Frozen in Time
by Owen Beattie and John Geiger 1987
(E.P. Dutton, U.S./ Bloomsbury Press, U.K./ Western Producer Prairie Books, Canada)
A fascinating account of Owen Beattie's scientific investigations into the fate of the Franklin expedition.

Polar Passage
by Jeff MacInnis with Wade Rowland 1989
(Ballantine Books, U.S./ Random House, Canada)
Jeff MacInnis tells the amazing story of how he and partner Mike Beedell made the first completely sail-powered journey across the Northwest Passage in their tiny catamaran from 1986 to 1988.

The Arctic World Series
by Bobbie Kalman 1988
(Crabtree Publishing Company, U.S., Canada)
Four colorful books—*The Arctic Land, Arctic Animals, Arctic Whales and Whaling* and *An Arctic Community*—describe the many aspects of modern life above the tree line.

Julie of the Wolves
Jean Craighead George 1972
(Harper & Row, U.S.)
Julie runs away from home and becomes lost in the Alaskan wilderness where she is accepted by a pack of wolves and lives with them as one of their own. A Newbery Award winner.